The Knowable Emotions

THE KNOWABLE EMOTIONS

poems

Heikki Huotari

LynxHousePress
Spokane, Washington

The present volume contains poems selected from each of three chapbooks: *Electrical and Spherical and Musical and Necessary,* which won the 2016 Gambling the Aisle chapbook contest; *Truth Table,* Finishing Line Press; and *Tooth and Shoe,* Willow Springs Books. Prior to their inclusion in the chapbooks versions of some of the poems appeared in the following journals:

Avatar Review: "Love's Lift," "Mother of Pearl," "Tautology is Grace"
Berkeley Poetry Review: "Reentry"
Coe Review: "Asymmetric," "Sleepstart"
Crazyhorse: "Small," "The Tenure of the Premise"
Diagram: "Ultraviolet"
Dual Coast Magazine: "Intrinsic"
Dime Show Review: "A Shoe In Each Of Two Canoes"
East Coast Literary Review: "The Color of Milk and Snow," "The Crossing"
Flexible Persona: "Cartwheel"
Fourteen Hills: "Between the Walls"
Fredericksburg Literary and Art Review: "Bucket"
The Hamilton Stone Review: "Proprioception," "You May Have Won Already," "In Addition"
Indefinite Space: "Nondestructive Testing," "Patent Pending"
The Inflectionist Review: "Level"
Jersey Devil Press: "The Dream Before the Frog"
Modern Poetry Quarterly Review: "Quantum Logic"
Noctua Review: "Rapid Eye Movement"
The Offbeat: "Equal and Opposite"
Pacifica Literary Review: "Doppler Shift"
Poetry Pacific: "Tooth and Shoe"
Poetry Quarterly: "Upgrade"
Petrichor: "Beauty Sleep"
Puerto del Sol: "You Will See Neutrinos," "What Happens on the Earth," "Only After"
Sein und Werden: "Saint Elmo's Fire"
Star 82: "The Tell"
The Starving Artist: "Double Negative"
The Stockholm Review of Literature: "In Retrospect the Act"
Stone Highway Review: "Once Removed"
The Vehicle: "Crop Circle," "One Good Reason"
Third Wednesday: "Inhale," "Lullaby"
Tipton Poetry Journal: "To A Fault"

FIRST EDITION

Cover art by Mariëlle van Aart-Coppes. *Saturday Morning,* acrylic paint on canvas.
    Other fine paintings by Mariëlle van Aart-Coppes can be found online at www.magicaldaydream.com.
Author Photo: Kay Bradner.
Book & Cover Design: Christine Holbert.

LYNX HOUSE PRESS books are distributed by the University of Washington Press, 4333 Brooklyn Avenue NE, Seattle, WA 98195-9570.

Library of Congress Cataloging-in-Publication Data is available from the Library of Congress.
ISBN 978-0-89924-164-7

CONTENTS

From TRUTH TABLE

From ELECTRICAL AND SPHERICAL
AND MUSICAL AND NECESSARY

RAPID EYE MOVEMENT

My bread is buttered on whatever side is down.
From each of eighteen wheels I'm shedding tread.
She loves another then she loves another not and
like the eye behind the patch, I'm on call always
but the heart opposed to mine needs be right only
once and if in altered states like Idaho, balloons
with polka dots are tied to fence posts, it's a girl or
it's a boy and not a final answer and the relatives
who greet me are the relatives who didn't have the
time of day for me in life.

Suppose you were to cover your eyes with your own two hands and count and ask, *Where's little Jennifer?* Then little Jennifer might take you at your word and reassure you, saying, *I'm right here.* Suppose you were to cover your eyes with your own two hands and say, *Guess who.* Suppose your oceans and your atmospheres then had among them one red sunset and they turned to you and you knew how to play the game and you knew what to do.

SAINT ELMO'S FIRE

My heart beat prematurely and my kiss went wide and I lost points. It was my leap-year birthday so I came home early to an incomplete surprise, no candles on the cake and my well-wishers incompletely hidden. Then I was in charge of natural selection and conducting electricity so I made sure my flatfish had both eyes on one side and I time-traveled there and when I touched my mother's hair it felt like lacquer. Yours is soft.

BEAUTY SLEEP

You took small bites of, then put back into the
heart-shaped box, the knowable emotions, one
of which was love and one of which was love
exclusively of me. And on the seventh day my glass
eye rolled away. And octopuses put their pants on
one leg at a time. And someone's mother said my
face would freeze that way and I said, in defiance,
Fine.

DOUBLE NEGATIVE

Were mine a double negative, a gargoyle with its tongue stuck out, black snow might not not fall. My future former friend might make to shake my hand but then withdraw the offer. Not to have the time of my life I know I must be this tall and to comedians who fall or have a dying mother, I say, *That's a good one, different,* and to antimatter, *Thank you for the alibi,* to anti-antimatter, *You should go ahead of me as I'm still thinking, you have money out and you know what you want.*

BUCKET

One partition is induced by an equivalence relation, then another, pink-striped petals fall, and when they're scalable and can be added, you can call them vectors, although technically they don't exist except in orbit, outer space. I can't change color yet—my camouflage consists of covering my own eyes. So, chameleon on paisley, peace-abiding passionately, *Where's your alibi?* I ask, and Turing-testing you, I'm vigorously shaking your ghost limb and, standing on the not-a-step, I see the second ladder. While I slept you dressed me. Pink striped petals fall and at the bottom of the page the print gets small.

DOPPLER SHIFT

My hotels come in waves and particles and wake-up calls and modified genetically, my body's soft and warm and round, and you can't tell if I'm a work of art or hanging upside down or rolling naked, painted on a canvas on the floor. When I put on my turtleneck my head gets started up a sleeve and marching bands are diving off the bridge of which I am the lonely troll, the never-ending nerve, and in dark doorways even homeless men are looking at their phones, their faces lit, inhaling oxygen, exhaling CO_2.

Science Daily says if I'm a man-made atom, given ribs, an Adam's apple, and stay nearer to the mirror than the other man-made atoms I will live ten times as long so I arrange my armies of imaginary friends in three dimensional arrays. Because I have no children and have never been in prison or a foxhole, I'm still free to disbelieve and I have three degrees of freedom, roll and pitch and yaw and nothing rotates quite like pie at night when I'm invisible in my gorilla suit and lucid and Madonna and I share an office while we're young, moonlighting as adjunct professors.

ULTRAVIOLET

Although the powers that be assert there's nothing
here to see, no crime in progress, no blood-spattered
aftermath, I know what learns to love me in the
ultraviolet will move and loom stochastically and
if I choose the numbers, when I win I'll share the
prize, as we've all thought of someone's birthday
and of perfect birthdays there's a limited supply.

IN RESTROSPECT THE ACT

In retrospect the act is ethical and any meadow
that the sun gets to may rise and we are start-
ups, we are fool's gold, from the cake down we
are naked, vacant, and the spring's restoring force
proportional to its displacement and the short
unwinding road. The color wheel throws off its
chains, increasing frequency to fibrillation. When
I call it flesh it tastes like chicken, rattlesnake to
be exact.

MOTHER OF PEARL

In the antisepsis of an atmosphere I hope and fear the touch of rubber glove on rubber sleeve, the warm and damp reprieve, and in starvation mode, past passion, jaws wired shut, I digest my own muscle tissue, drink and breathe and see as through a reed, and I'm the source of light, the beauty queen appended to the float composed of chicken wire and tissue paper and, my candy thrown, my kisses blown, irrelevant, I'm iridescent.

LICENSE

If Superman can find a phone booth, God will authorize a big red essence. Waiting for the doors to open, nature loves a vacuum, loves the rush of air and swirl of leaves, and there are surely bioluminescent cuticles in edifices of inverted circles, me in there and you out here where radius associates with ray and honesty's blind prospectors parade and, given increments of mercy, millimeters, from Samaritans, I'm good to go, to go it on my own, so no more milk and cookies, Satan, no more staying up all night for you!

PROPRIOCEPTION

According to my inner ear's accelerometer, I'm sidling, there's time dilation and it's twelve A.M., so I know where my limbic system and my limbic system's children are and I don't need to see them. I'm abundantly supplied with gravity and subtlety and vibrate sympathetically with spiders at all angles, the excited plasma in the cursive tube of glass. The writing in the window says, *If you would have me, stay*. If you would have me stay then signal visibly and audibly and at the school bus and train crossing have your red and yellow fiberglass reflective arm descend.

YOU MAY HAVE WON ALREADY

When neither frying pan nor fire suffices, neither beds of glowing coals nor nails, the lilies of the field spin in in needing neither your liturgical consideration nor your statutory spatial frame. How beautiful, beneath the vees of geese, the lessons learned, how visible the pick-up sticks and stitches and how radial the pedals there for metric feet to step on: singing, living, status quo.

This offer ends at midnight: love me, love my latitude and longitude and altitude, agree with me, and I'll throw in a fourth dimension absolutely free.

TO A FAULT

What stops moving relative to you you ought to take for granted. There are more than fifty volatile organic compounds in that new car smell. When you're a microscopic hammer all you see are microscopic nails. Your sisters' hammers live three thousand miles away. You're vertical and ethical and when you gun your egg-shaped outboard engine, you'll be juxtaposing no tectonic plates and towing none of California out to sea.

PARTIALLY INFORMED

Is there anything I could not make of glass and
squeeze the blood from? Is it day yet? Are there
colors? Is there weather? It may be the product of
the tree of knowledge that I bought and thought
was fruit and then the weapon I was cleaning I
thought wasn't loaded. Now I'll have my partially
informed opinion in a semi tractor, on the freeway
with no entrances or exits, in my slipstream, with
one wall of flapping plastic, half a home.

YOU WILL SEE NEUTRINOS

Start your engines, synchronize your watches, purify your scintillators—you will see neutrinos, you will on occasion have an interaction. Per the CPR instructor, those you save successfully will thank you when you break their ribs. Subtract a saxophone and add a planet and be one of many clowns and tumble out and run around and juggle. Juggle flaming chainsaws. Have that fascinating public conversation with yourself.

WHAT HAPPENS ON THE EARTH

Now what happens on the earth stays on the earth. The shadow of the minaret is densely packed with pilgrims. Hypnagogic pilot, will you speak? My pigs are winged and Greek. So many things are not yet known! Imagine how sea urchins feel, no sooner off the ocean floor than in non-stop negotiation, and imagine, having seen neutrinos, you become a better person.

ONLY AFTER

Only after you have put your own invisibility cloak on should you attempt to help with mine. I'll handle truth and then I'll handle hot potatoes. Stipulations are proliferating but I know if I keep turning pages I will finally find a place to sign, so blindfold and supply me with corsage and pin and spin me seven times and tell me when I'm warm and when I'm cold and what I'm thinking, that I'm wrong and that you wouldn't recognize me even if you saw me in your sleep.

FIRST LIGHT

First-light stalactites and stalagmites mingle and my striped horizon narrows to an edge, a precipice, a light behind. I mean for your last dream to be of flying and affix transparent wings. I promise you more music and less talk. Don't touch that dial and I'll beguile you with a total absence of dead air. So you can swivel childlike in your chair, I'll put on Wagner's never-ending Ring, and I'll run interference for you, be your crumple zone, and suddenly you'll trust me.

SHORT CIRCUIT

By the law of the excluded middle either this world
is my home or not. Cicadas buzz because they
can't fluoresce. Cicadas tune to my tinnitus and
where one's electrical and spherical and musical
and necessary any cast of thousands may suffice
and when I look into my convex mirror I will
know that I'm infallible, inflexible, and when I
need them I'll have documents by which for every
day of work or school I miss I'll be excused.

IN ADDITION

I believe it when I fail to see it & when I think it is best & then there's poetry in stasis & then Mother Nature loves a vacuum & someone dispensable to taste the food & I see people pray & faint at altitude & miracles occur in my vicinity & I'm a saint & see right through you & a clock that gains two minutes every day is right approximately once a month & in my flightless bird's-eye view maybe if I hold my breath you will love me before I turn blue.

THE TELL

The fasteners that hold my parts together turn but
one way and but once and I will void my warranty
should I but try to fight it. Like the Google car
that can't negotiate a four-way stop I'm too polite.

My secret guilty pleasure is derivative however
close I hold my cards, however, simulating bells,
in post and rope and canvas corners into yellow
plastic buckets I spit out however many false,
misleading teeth.

The self serve copier is jammed, the workroom
door ajar, the self at home and watching Law and
Order reruns and lamenting that on technicalities
the perpetrators always walk.

INTRINSIC

Maybe there are two of you and you have yet to separate or you're disoriented, morally opposed to gravity and gender neutral in a unitard and showing evidence of neither pin nor stitch nor seam and maybe some day you'll be fully centrally symmetric, warm and sleeping peacefully—through bending, stretching, twisting, your geometry may be intrinsic, rain resistant, never change.

ONCE REMOVED

Once in motion, one accelerates to make the yellow light. What one runs after is a hat and though the music of the spheres has stopped, we're moving still together as on ice, as if moon lit. What keeps us going? One of us is saved and one is spoken for. For each of us there is that first night. On the second night we trade.

And then there's temperature and pressure and the weave of rebar in concrete; you offer me a midnight knife, the kind that saws a radiator hose in half then slices a tomato paper thin; you tell me how and when to pray and I say, *Bring the plastic masks and rubber crutches on and take those broken things away.*

From TRUTH TABLE

SMALL

When the moon throws photons at me I can step down into any open grave and when my black earth bulges, I can finally learn to fly and when the past outgrows its planter, I can give the future one more try. If you take all the covers, then I'm free to find another bed or room or house in which to sleep. But when I'm squeezed from both sides, painted in a corner with my back against the wall, I only can be small, as in a Middle-Ages painting, as a child with adult features, standing on my mother's lap, and small.

THE COLOR OF MILK AND SNOW

Sticks to pick their sticks up, stars and scars crisscrossing, given to reflect on, neither transmit nor absorb and wisdom teeth extracted, scrimshawed, sharpened, road-side signs of microscopic cubic corners, compound eyes that shine and, happy hour long since past, last call, and suddenly we've overstayed our welcome and the barmaid's flipping on and off the lights and crooning *Closing. You don't have to go home but you can't stay here.*

THE TENURE OF THE PREMISE

I'll be sorry in advance and at the square dance, back to back, I'll trade my grief and guilt for yours. The next event will feature spooning, spinning, chinning, tossing, nosing or the finding, in green grass, of colored eggs, and at this contest everybody wins, as life is fair. A leg that's barely there puts on a foot with seven toes. Now vertical and merrier and more, we disco on a window on the floor, our cause is probable and just and in our creaky hearses, from our mildewed hymnals, we will sing of all things sweet and sour and from a sea of ink an artificial chicken drinks. Our logic takes us anywhere we want to go and still about our central premise, not one question has been raised.

QUANTUM LOGIC

A radius, a play of chain, a turn of phrase, a thought balloon, a thought balloon is red and round or red not round or round not red or neither red nor round. A thought balloon, when tweaked and twisted, is a poodle or a hat or both a poodle and a hat, a tag team, alternately one a flying fish and one a prehistoric horse. You are my forty days and forty nights of rain. You are my favorite raft of ants. Don't tell the other rafts of ants I said so.

CROP CIRCLE

Every moment spawns a watershed of dialects and rights of way and self-inflicted priests. In every window pane the face of night, the little bottle that we share, and that we are. They're topologically equivalent, the donut and the coffee cup, with each a glaze and each a glint and each a coil of steam. There's prerecorded laughter. Trusting, faithful, all fall back. The landing wheels, just lowered, turn, to no avail, in air. The flying saucer spins into a field of wheat and they, the aliens, the mischief makers, they have elementary tools and ropes and wires and boards tied to their feet.

BETWEEN THE WALLS

Between the walls were pipes and wires and statements made of nails and waterfalls of consciousness and we went over in our barrels, in our naked bankrupt's barrels, in suspenders, staves and hoops, and we were intricate and octopi embracing beak to beak and suction cup to suction cup and every tentacle a brain.

ONE GOOD REASON

An ice cream truck is playing Mary Had a Little Lamb and all God's oats are wild, each night the first, tomorrow God goes off to war. I say to God, *I thought you said your Virgin Mary doesn't bite,* God says, *It's not my Virgin Mary. Anyway it's just a nibble cause she likes you and she wants to play.* And in her ransom note, the Virgin Mary writes, *I have your dream, and if you want to see your dream again you'll do exactly as I say.*

LOVE'S LIFT

By the scattered feathers and the black-tape
outline you will know me, by raised footprints of
compacted snow, and one foot in a bathtub, one
in bed, a shoe in each of two canoes, electrified,
vibrating, secret spent, I may repent, inhaling
steam and chained to my machine through swing
and graveyard shift and balanced on a fence post
while Delilah, laughing, drives away, I'll stick my
head and neck out, legs and pointed tail, and I'll
be swimming in the air. Because I once was loved I
am of worth. I pity those poor turtles who imagine
they're still holding up the earth.

LULLABY

Curse the darkness. Damn the candle. In one eye
and out the other goes the light and an hallucination
turns your head and when you stumble, drunk on
love, tattoos her name somewhere on you and
now you're sitting at the children's table making
airplanes of gray plastic fragments and evaporating
glue.

TAUTOLOGY IS GRACE

In my cone of streetlight, on my slanting slab of concrete, in my three-wheeled shopping cart a trusting puppy and a hubcap and an amber tail light lens, I'll be some family's pants, some party's life, mistake a lampshade for a hat and when the music stops at sunrise and I'm crawling on the freeway, banners on highrises tell me if I lived here I would now be home.

UPGRADE

Born in sin, you must love someone: you may cast
the second stone. Past lives, a body in each room
and none to blame. Another day, another cake and
teeth on necklaces that we may hold our heads up
without shame, that we may hold our heads up
without shame.

INHALE

Iguanas freeze and lose their grips and fall like fruit from trees, like bricks, and during earthquakes knees and buildings learn to flex and breathe and in a vortex of low pressure clowns and clown enablers scratch and stretch and yawn and when I die a second time I'll take the spiral candles from my cake and send my parents back to jail and when they ask me to withdraw my wishes I'll inhale.

ASYMMETRIC

At the other altar, Abelard says *Now I don't.*
Therefore what God has put asunder let no man
or woman or third person join. A hammer rotates,
peen and claw and handle, in slow motion by my
window on the freeway, on the freeway when a
flower over one ear means a thousand nights of
bliss, the other, come within ten feet and die.

THE CROSSING

If ever there were rivers they've gone underground. Another day, another dry oasis, mirage, scaffold, branch of bone, first fish with feet, a solid, salt and sand, and take our belts and shoes and wave us through. Kidnapped and hand to handed, we are less an island than an island shaped by waves and in our robes, our wedding black and white, we're serenaded, fireflies and five sizes of guitar, and when the distance between us increases it must be that at least one of us is feverish and freezing, throwing clothes off in the snow.

The panda's face resembles mine more than the octopus's does and to be taken for a ride, the octopus must be this flexible, the octopus must be this tall. Until that time, the octopus may be a terrorist or narcissist, a narcissist who'd rather talk about the narcissist than me. I am an ant that's basking in your magnifying glass, your ingenuity and empathy and tentacles of dentistry—one holds a mirror like a spoon and one a color-coded imitation tooth.

SLEEPSTART

Because the thing you try to lift is not as heavy as you thought it flies up in the air, a step is taken from you when you step, except what you expect to step on isn't there and God throws down his bike right at the bottom of the stairs and when you say to Him, *Someone will fall,* He says, *Let them take care.*

REENTRY

The astronauts are sleeping, their possessions, wallets, bullets, coins and keys on distant dressers, carry-ons in bins above their heads. The astronauts are sleeping in the shadow of the earth and in their wings and in their pods and soft and warm and white. The astronauts are sleeping in their cars, their cardboard boxes on concrete. The astronauts are sleeping while I pace and while I age and while I set the breakfast table. After their pajama party, having whispered, tickled, giggled half the night, now finally they're asleep but soon they'll be awake and tumble with their precious laughter down the stairs.

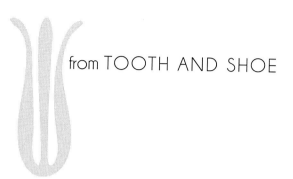

from TOOTH AND SHOE

TURN THE FLORA AND THE FAUNA OFF

Turn the flora and the fauna and the automatic pilot off and be like children. Jettison your adult things. If Mother Nature has a daughter Mother Nature's daughter is a hammer or a shoe and you may stage a play and walk away and if you bring the house down you may get another house and try again and you may see the me in you as virtue. If I'm satisfied or qualified or show remorse release me on my own recognizance but if I'm neither satisfied nor qualified nor show remorse, erect a chain-link fence for me to grab and rattle—may I make my statement safely in the designated protest zone.

KICK TURN

From the dark unconscious I track paint into a
concrete cubic corner and my footsteps echo and
the noise machines of spirit guides enable me and
I have half a mind to be a cortical homunculus
with outsized lips and thumbs and suddenly I'm
operating on a tilting oval table, and I'm saying I
will be the doctor now.

APOTHEOSIS

We say smoke em if you got em, this may take a while and meanwhile you may occupy a time and place and inhale molecules of nitrogen and oxygen and may be filmed before that great green screen and then your background swapped for something like the Eiffel Tower. Now your righteousness is artificially enhanced and in both book of life and hall of fame there is a glowing golden asterisk beside your name—in heaven as on earth you'll be the lucky millionth customer, the only ever customer whose money we don't need.

LEVEL

The bubble on the level centers when compassion
matches strategy, magnetic north is true, all ice
confined to Greenland and all axes of rotation
stable, not rotating end on end as hollow bones do
and the glass of iridescent water on the counter set
to vibrate gently when there is a message from the
oscillating infrastructure of the earth.

CONTROL GROUP

The essential chemical constituent is synthesized under conditions replicating those of early earth, extruded, pressed into the shapes of animals and served up to the criminals, but not the kind we like. The kind we like are put up in hotels and given new identities, careers and social skills and can have anything they want delivered to their doors for their last meals. We leave the lights on for them and their catwalks are square circles so whichever way they turn at any of their intersections they are almost home.

TOOTH AND SHOE

You might have nibbled on an earlobe when that earlobe and you both were soft and warm but now when clowns collide the comical atomic particles fly off in all directions, now the universe is largely laughing matter. Guess which shoe the tooth is in, which tooth is in the shoe and which is tooth and which is shoe and spin your web of ethics, close your eyes and feel the dented fender, be the dented fender, be the dent.

MOVED BY SOMETHING SMALL

I live so everything that's iced might finally die
and to be moved by something small, to think it's
my idea. Now the cup of hormone-laden milk is
closer or the artificial arm is longer than the little
man in me had thought. Therefore you'll validate
me sympathetically, and having seen my proof of
purchase you'll approve one out-of-body flight
and, like the insect's opposite, my inside hard and
outside soft, I'll don civilian clothes and scurry to
the nearest crack of dawn.

NONDESTRUCTIVE TESTING

The moon would be a mirror were it not a
paper plate, a window were it not a window
in a warehouse with a grate and if I own the
microscope, the microscope has never bitten me or
I have never seen the microscope before today I'll
say, My microscope won't bite and I'll just sit here
in the dark, deracinate, defenestrate and snap the
handle off the pot and dump the goulash in the
fire. My subconscious says I'm worse than naked
if in public in my underwear and last night's ashes
in my hair and I'm your final wife. One moment
more of silence for my hero brings my hero back
to life.

PATENT PENDING

Perpetual Emotion® does not contradict the laws of nature & Perpetual Emotion® is the blissful myth of multitudes of multitudes & each of seven plans of doctors of philosophy is practical & if the laws of nature are suspended each of seven doctors of philosophy will have a year's supply of oxygen in canisters to breathe.

CARTWHEEL

If I'm sewing anecdotes together autonomically and ambiguity and antigravity take over I just spin the other way. If I forget the object's name I say, *the thing with wheels, the thing with wheels,* and now I mean it—now that wheels are reinvented wheels are everywhere and anything with wheels with me will be OK.

THE CENTER

We have promises to break and all the time we need and all the scenes of crime we need to keep us elevated while we stay awake. This floor goes half-way up the wall—how many floors can you say that about? Disposing of our better angels we'll be equal, hate mortality then love mortality then nod to both sides, and when one of us becomes a man, a one-man band, he'll circumvent the law of the excluded middle and in reconciling antithetical emotions have a pretend tantrum and set fire to his air guitar.

CHAMELEON ON PAISLEY

If it's microscopic in a viscous liquid and has neon green and pink flagella flapping, it might just be my food's food. To verify our alibi they're taking each of us to separate rooms and asking each of us which tire was flat. The angel of this incident is but a shadow of the angel of recrimination—once the mental map's unfolded there's no going back.

TOOTH AND SPOON

The panda's face resembles mine more than the octopus's does and to be taken for a ride, the octopus must be this flexible, the octopus must be this tall. Until that day, the octopus may be a terrorist or narcissist, a narcissist who'd rather speak about the narcissist than me and, speaking of the tentacles of dentistry, one holds a mirror like a spoon and one a new ceramic tooth.

EQUAL AND OPPOSITE

One of these two things is different from the other therefore one of these two things does not belong—in an interior a spiny antibody met a spiny anti-antibody then the one that won was swinging nonchalantly from a chandelier or stood corrected on a pedestal, depending on which way the wind was blowing, one demoted, one promoted—I was wrong and you were right or vice versa.

GRACE

Some optic nerve you have running down a cinder cone and taking steps knee-deep in scree and seeing to or after images of clouds about the moon and thinking you have without asking anything of anybody stood your ground and like the omnivore you are you'll eat whatever is put on your plate and like the cat you are will know the mouse though injured will for your amusement live forever.

STOPPING DISTANCE

These hominids have contradicting thumbs—
some put an end to misery and some prolong it.
The odd petal tells me I am to be loved. When
disbelievers' red suspenders hold believers' pants
up, Jesus in his formal throes will be an after-
market mullion and will equally divide the light.
Now here is the ado and further here is the ado
that up to now you've had to do without.

YOUR PLACEBO, TRULY

Push my buttons in the proper sequence and I'll change. My camouflage will automatically adjust. Your camouflage will automatically adjust. I'm here to tell you you exist just when you're passing between me and my true purpose, my demise, and slightly dim the light, and in my semi-privacy, with my prognosis my profession, I'll be your attractive nuisance, I'll say, *Come on in, the water's fine.*

A SHOE IN EACH OF TWO CANOES

In a pigsty or an afterlife I will not pay to stay but neither will I pay to leave. Beneath what was a sometime streetlight there's a shattering of glass and both sides do it, birds as well as bees, and when I feel the rigor mortis coming on, I'll hop across the double time line like a pair of pairs of rabbits, amber lights and pearly gates be damned.